MW01121333

SPOTLIGHT ON
THE BRITISH RAJ

William Golant

SPOTLIGHT ON HISTORY

Cover illustration: A British resident presides over a musical performance.

Editor: Deborah Elliott

First published in 1988 by Wayland (Publishers) Ltd
61 Western Road, Hove, East Sussex BN3 1JD, England

© Copyright 1988 Wayland (Publishers) Ltd

British Library Cataloguing in Publication Data

Golant, William
   Spotlight on the British Raj. —
   (Spotlight on history).
   1. India — History — British
   occupation 1765–1947 — Juvenile
   literature
   I. Title
   954.03   DS463

   ISBN 1-85210-088-5

Typeset, printed and bound in the UK at The Bath Press, Avon

CONTENTS

1 INDIA, A SUB-CONTINENT

At midnight on 15 August 1947, Lord Mountbatten, the last viceroy of India, announced the end of the British Raj. Even at this late hour, about half a million people jammed the streets of New Delhi to parade, and shout. Everyone understood that this evening, described by Mountbatten as 'the most remarkable and inspiring day' of his life, was an important moment in history. Two new nations, India and Pakistan, were about to be born while the Empire of a third nation, Great Britain, was coming to an end. British rule in India, known as the Raj from the Hindi word ruler, had lasted for two centuries.

A jubilant crowd greets Lord and Lady Mountbatten during the celebrations which marked the end of the British Raj.

At 8.30 am on 15 August 1947, Jawaharlal Nehru, the first prime minister of free India, was sworn in by Lord Mountbatten.

A gamble on the rain

India is an impressive and beautiful country. It has a coastline of 3,000 miles and a land mass as large as Europe, excluding the USSR. The Himalayas are the highest mountain chain in the world and have for centuries, acted as a barrier against invading armies. The immense snow-covered mountains feed the great rivers of the Indus and the Ganges. Throughout the history of India, the fertile region of the Indus valley has been the centre of wealth and government.

India's mainly dry and hot climate is dramatically interrupted between June and October by monsoon rains. The prosperity of many Indian people depends on these rains, which can be either insufficient or too heavy. In 1876, during a heavy downpour, approximately 100,000 people died in only half an hour. The Indian farmer, or *ryot*, is constantly threatened by drought and flood, his livelihood depending on the rains. The name India is actually derived from Indra, the Hindu god of rain, thunder and lightning.

9

Invaders who stayed

Invaders came to India through the mountain passes in the north-western Himalayas in search of wealth. The Aryans began to conquer northern India in about 2000 BC. They used the classical language of Sanskrit to develop the Hindu religion. They introduced the *Rigveda* and two epic poems, the *Mahabharata* and the *Ramayana*, which became masterpieces of world literature. The Aryans also developed a new social system to help them govern the Indian people. By dividing the population into castes everyone was assigned a specific position in society.

Apart from the Aryan priests or Brahmins, who had the greatest authority, there were three other castes: the warriors, the merchants, and the farmers. The poorest workers were the 'outcastes', or untouchables. Many centuries later, the Indian leader Mahatma Gandhi opposed the prejudice against the untouchables and called them *harijans* meaning 'children of God'.

An earlier critic of the caste system was Siddartha Gautama (560–480 BC) who renounced his wealth and family to become a poor traveller in search of spiritual peace. He taught the value of reason, purity and experience, and was the founder of the Buddhist religion.

Every year throughout their history, the livelihood of many Indian people has been threatened by monsoon rains which cause severe flooding.

A statue of Alexander the Great, who, together with his armies, raided India in 326 BC.

Empires

By the time Alexander the Great raided India in 326 BC, it was a country famous for its fine cloth, perfumes, precious stones, gold jewellery, and steel swords. The Indian king, Chandragupta, expelled the Greeks in 305 BC and organized the Maurya Empire (322–185 BC). His grandson Asoka (273–232 BC), the most famous Indian king, conquered nearly two thirds of the country. The slaughter he witnessed in the battlefields filled the warrior-king with shame and he decided to become a Buddhist. Wishing to inspire his country, Asoka built pillars with moral inscriptions such as, 'Thus saith His Majesty: "Father and mother must be obeyed; similarly respect for living creatures must be enforced; truth must be spoken."'

11

A nineteenth-century illustration shows the Indian leader, Porus, opposing Alexander in 326 BC, *with an army of elephants.*

A second Empire flourished under the Guptas (320–647 AD) when Indian culture reached a golden age in art, music, science, industry and philosophy. The Guptas invented the decimal system and established the zero as a unit of measurement.

The wealth and achievements of India lured other invaders over the next thousand years. The Greeks, Kusghans and Huns from central Asia crossed into India in an attempt to plunder some of the wealth. In 712, India was unsuccessfully invaded by Arab followers of Islam. A second invasion occurred in 1175, and then in 1398 Tamerlane and his Tartar army from central Asia attacked India.

In 1206 Turkish Muslims finally conquered the Punjab and ruled as Sultans of Delhi until 1526, when Babur, a relative of Genghis Khan, became the first Mogul Emperor. In his memoirs, Babur revealed that he found India to be a country of few charms. One day while eating a melon he experienced 'a strong sense of loneliness and a sense of exile from my native country; and I could not help shedding tears while I was eating it.'

Mogul rule established an elaborate court which survived until 1761. In 1652, the Mogul Emperor, Shahajan, grandson of Asoka built the Taj Mahal, one of the most beautiful and famous buildings in the world. He built it to honour the grace and beauty of his favourite wife.

After two centuries of constant warfare between the Hindu rulers and their Muslim invaders, an uneasy relationship existed between them. Under Babur's grandson, Akbar (1542–1605), the Hindu

Babur, who was the first Mogul Emperor of India between 1526 and 1530.

The beautiful, marble Taj Mahal was built in 1652 by the Mogul Emperor, Shahajan, in memory of his beloved wife Mumtaz Mahal.

population was allowed to practice its religious beliefs and retain its ancient customs. Although the Mogul empire was despotic, it was not able to control the whole of India.

India, a new El Dorado

The European invasion of India did not come through the mountains but from the sea. By the end of the fifteenth century, Europeans believed India to be a place of fabulous wealth. In 1492 Christopher Columbus sailed from Cadiz in Spain in search of a western route to India, but it was Vasco da Gama who arrived in India in 1498 and established a Portuguese trading station on the west coast (Goa). The Portugese were soon followed by the Dutch, the French and the English.

In his play, *Merry Wives of Windsor*, William Shakespeare suggests the Elizabethan impression of India. Falstaff has convinced himself that Mistressess Ford and Page are in love with him and since they control the purse strings of their households, he hopes for both excitement and profit. 'They shall be my East and West Indies and I shall trade with them both.' A few years later, in 1600, the East India Company of London was given a royal charter for the exclusive right to trade in the East.

2 EMPIRE BUILDING

In 1600 Queen Elizabeth I granted a group of London merchants the exclusive right to trade in the East. This meant that no other British company could ship goods from the Far East to Britain. Merchants organized trading voyages to the Spice Islands (in present day Indonesia) because of the high price of spices, especially pepper, on the London market. Because the trade monopoly given by the Queen to the East India Company, as it was called, did not apply to the trading companies of the Portuguese in India and the Dutch in Indonesia, competition and rivalry were inevitable.

The private army of the East India Company practising drill at its Bombay Green headquarters.

One of the carracks (sailing ships) used by the East India Company to transport cargoes of merchandise.

At first the East India Company used India solely as a port to supply their ships and to buy Indian cotton to sell in the Spice Islands. When the East India Company met with fierce opposition from the powerful Dutch in Indonesia, it decided to concentrate on India. In 1615 Sir Thomas Roe was sent as an ambassador to the court of the Great Mogul at Agra, where he received permission to open trading stations in India. He wrote to London that the Company should avoid involvement in the political and military affairs of this strange country. 'Let this be received as a rule that if you will profit, seek it at sea, and in quiet trade; for without controversy, it is an error to affect garrisons and land wars in India.' This advice was followed for the next seventy years. Cargoes of cotton and indigo (a deep-blue dye), silk, handwoven cloth, pepper, saltpetre (used for gunpowder), and medicines regularly arrived in Britain. Meanwhile, the princes of the Indian courts bought chandeliers, coaches, silver and mirrors from Britain.

The East India Company made exceptionally high profits from its Indian trade. The number of trading stations, called factories, quickly increased. By 1647, the East India Company had twenty-three factories in operation with ninety-nine employees. During the seventeenth century, the main factories became the walled forts of St George in Bengal, Fort William in Madras, and Bombay Castle, around which India's major towns developed.

Transport ships belonging to the East India Company sailing into Bombay harbour to be unloaded at one of the many Company factories.

Diamond Pitt, the nabob

Englishmen soon learned that fabulous wealth could be made in India. Those who returned to England after making their fortune in India were known as *nabobs*. The career of Thomas Pitt (1653–1726), founder of the Pitt dynasty—'a family as considerable as any'—was impressive by any standards.

Pitt came to India as a teenager. He did not pay any attention to the East India Company's monopoly and sold Indian goods throughout Asia. He returned to England a very rich man, and became member of Parliament for New Sarum in 1689. He was so powerful that the East India Company gave up trying to bring him to court for illegal trading. Instead, he was asked to become Governor of Madras. He never grew tired of making money and in 1701 he bought a fabulous uncut diamond weighing 410 carats for £20,000 which he sold to the French Royal family for £35,000. From then on he was known as 'Diamond Pitt'.

Conquerors

During the eighteenth and nineteenth centuries, the East India Company became less involved with trade and began to conquer and administer more and more of India. In 1707, the death of Aurangzeb, the Mogul Emperor, threw the country into a century of civil war. The East India Company trained Indian troops, hired a navy, and developed its own army to support Indian princes who could either pay the Company or be of some service.

A view of the Esplanade in Calcutta. Many of the European settlers chose cities such as Calcutta as their new homes and tried to impose European culture on the people of India.

Robert Clive, the general and statesman, whose victory against Siraj-ud-Daula's army at Plassey in 1757, succeeded in strengthening British rule in India.

Prior to 1756, the French, who were enemies of Britain in Europe and America, had attempted to establish a permanent base in India. Rather than be removed by French competitors, the East India Company helped those princes who opposed the French and their allies. This policy was so effective that French imperial ambitions in India collapsed.

Robert Clive (1725–1774) was a clerk with the East India Company in Madras. He obtained a commission in the Company's army and proved himself to be a brilliant soldier. In 1756 the nawab, or ruler, over Bengal, Siraj-ud-Daula, attacked the British settlement in

The incident known as the Black Hole of Calcutta, where almost 146 British people were imprisoned by Siraj-ud-Daula in 1756. Almost all died of suffocation.

Calcutta. Of the 146 defenders who were imprisoned in the infamous Black Hole of Calcutta, a room 5.5 m by 4.6 m, almost all died from suffocation on the first night. Clive was called upon to revenge the outrage and joined with other Indian princes in opposition to Siraj-ud-Daula. With 1,000 European troops and 2,000 sepoys (Indian soldiers), he defeated Siraj-ud-Daula's inefficient army of 60,000 at the battle of Plassey in 1757.

Clive received large cash rewards from the grateful Indian princes. He became governor of Bengal and gained the right to govern the whole territory of Bengal for the East India Company. When he returned to England he was charged with unfairly adding to his personal fortune. He successfully defended himself before Parliament in 1772 when he declared: 'I stand astonished at my own moderation.'

Warren Hastings (1732–1818) became the first governor general of India. During his period of office from 1773 to 1785, a time when the American colonies rebelled against Great Britain, British control over Indian territory increased. Indian princes paid the East India Company money and tributes in return for the security which British military power gave them.

Warren Hastings laid the foundations for British rule over the whole of India, by introducing law courts and a civil service to administer the country. He also tried to forbid the practice of thuggee, in which gangs of robbers attacked travellers—this is the origin of the English word thug. However, as a result of increasing British territory in India, Hastings made enemies in Britain. Like Clive, he was brought to trial before the House of Lords in 1784. Though acquitted, the trial lasted seven years and Hastings lost all his wealth in paying the legal costs.

Indians awaiting trial being guarded by a Nujeeb policeman (right). One of Warren Hastings' policies, whilst in office, was to outlaw the practice of thugee, *which involved gangs of criminals robbing travellers.*

A cartoon showing Warren Hastings, the first governor general of India, on his official elephant.

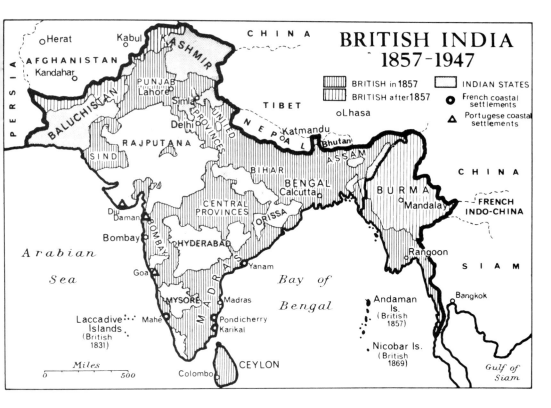

The above map illustrates the different territories within India which were occupied by the British, French and Portuguese between 1857 and 1947.

During the nineteenth century, Britain acquired large portions of India through conquest. Burma and the Punjab were annexed during the Burma wars of 1824, 1852 and 1885. The Sind was added to British India in 1843 and the Sikh wars of 1845 and 1849 brought yet more territory. Not everyone in Britain was happy about these conquests, however. The trials of Clive and Hastings showed that Parliament disliked the way in which the East India Company, a private company, had taken over the functions of government. In 1773 Parliament began to regulate the Company and after 1793 the Company's charter had to be renewed every twenty years. In 1833 the East India Company ended all trading activities and by 1853 it was reduced to merely acting in trust for Parliament, though for no fixed period. The rule of the East India Company did not survive the Sepoy Mutiny of 1857.

3 THE JEWEL IN THE CROWN

The Sepoy Mutiny

The East India Company's Indian army had approximately 233,000 sepoys. In 1852 the Enfield rifle was brought from Britain for use by the sepoys. The rifle used a special cartridge which was greased with pig and cow fat to keep the gunpowder dry. The end of the cartridge had to be bitten off before the ball and powder could be pushed down the barrel of the gun. As the cow is sacred to Hindus and the pig is regarded as unclean by Muslims, the sepoys rebelled.

A group of Indian Sepoys from the East India Company's Indian army at Lucknow in 1857.

Fighting between rebel Sepoys and the British, in the streets of Delhi, during the Sepoy Mutiny in 1857.

Eighty-five sepoys were arrested at Meerut in Bengal in May 1857 for refusing to use the cartridges. Their friends attacked the barracks and released the prisoners. The rebels then marched 64 km to Delhi and overran the town. Worse followed when after capturing Delhi the rebels, now led by Nana Sahib, pressed on to Cawnpore. The British forces held out against them for three weeks but finally surrendered. Though promised safe conduct when they gave themselves up, the soldiers, their wives and children were all massacred. The rebels then captured Lucknow.

After this event anger spread from India to Britain and the massacre at Lucknow marked the beginning of a new kind of suspicion by the British towards Indians. Troops sent out from Britain were joined by loyal sepoys from the Punjab and Madras, and the rebellion was soon

The Sepoy Mutiny was a bloody event in the history of the Raj. Many soldiers and their wives and children were massacred.

A contemporary drawing illustrating the massacre at Lucknow in 1857, during the Sepoy Mutiny.

suppressed. By 1859 the towns which had fallen to the rebels had been retaken. As a result of the Sepoy Mutiny, however, the East India Company was abolished and Parliament assumed direct control of Indian affairs.

Queen Victoria, Empress of India

Parliamentary control of India occurred at around the same time that Britain increased its wealth and power. Britain's dominant position in the world seemed closely linked to her control over India. In 1869 the Suez Canal was opened and the shorter distance between Britain and India led to increased trade. India soon became the centre of a trading empire which stretched to China, Japan, and Australia. A large and efficient navy was built, by the British, to carry goods and people as well as to defend the Empire. One-fifth of Britain's total foreign investment went to India as did many British exports, especially cotton and machinery.

Queen Victoria who was officially proclaimed Empress of India by act of Parliament in 1876.

Queen Victoria wanted to become Empress of India. After all, Britain's European rivals, the King of Prussia and the Tsar of Russia were called Emperors. In matters of protocol it was embarrassing for the Queen of England to be below these weaker rulers. She complained to her secretary in 1873: 'I am an Empress and in common conversation am sometimes called Empress of India. Why have I never officially assumed this title? I feel I ought to do so.' Prime Minister Disraeli, who usually tried to please as well as amuse his Queen, agreed. Besides satisfying Victoria's desire to be Empress, he saw that this new title was a useful symbol of British greatness and determination to rule India.

In 1876 Queen Victoria was officially proclaimed Empress by act of Parliament. She loved signing her name Victoria Regina et Imperatrix (Queen and Empress) and planned to have a troop of Sikh cavalry come to Britain as a special guard of honour. Towards the end of her life Queen Victoria began studying Hindi in order to achieve a better understanding of the people she governed.

The white man's burden

Victorian society was moral and practical and for the next forty years the British tried to justify the Raj by claiming that they had gone to India out of moral kindness. The paternalistic and imperialist attitude of the British is shown in a poem by Rudyard Kipling (1865–1936).

'Take up the white man's burden
Send forth the best ye breed–
Go bind your sons to exile
To serve your captive's need;
To wait in heavy harness
On fluttered folk and wild–
Your new-caught, sullen people,
Half-devil and half-child.'

Born in Bombay, Kipling was attracted by the exotic splendours of India. He also believed that the British had to keep their distance from the country they had come to govern. Many of his Indian stories and poems are about the conflict between the attractiveness of India and his belief in the need to defend British values. His novel *Kim* is the story of a British boy who is brought up by Indian foster parents. Though he looks like an Indian, the boy eventually learns that he must think and act like a sahib.

Rudyard Kipling, the English poet, short-story writer and novelist whose novel Kim *dealt with the subject of the British presence in India.*

Progress

Britain benefited greatly from governing India. India provided soldiers for a large army, a market for British goods, supplies of raw materials, and the prestige of governing a subcontinent. The benefits to the Indian people were that the British introduced a common language (English) which united different peoples. They also introduced British principles of government along with western science and modern technology.

After the Sepoy Mutiny, however, the British were frequently troubled about how long their control over India would last and what exactly their aims concerning India were. They resisted their own

One of the lasting benefits of the Raj was the construction of an efficient railway system.

The Victoria Railway Terminus in Bombay was built in 1887. It was a symbol of Victorian confidence in the Raj.

uncertainty by stressing that there was something noble and constructive in the relationship. They cited the expansion of the Indian railways as an example of how India was clearly benefiting from British rule.

The railways
In 1869 the Government of India began to build railways throughout the country. The immense size of India coupled with the difficult landscape made this a great engineering achievement. Over one hundred tunnels were needed for the 96.6 km track through the mountains outside Bombay. At one place on the Ganges, ninety-three bridges were

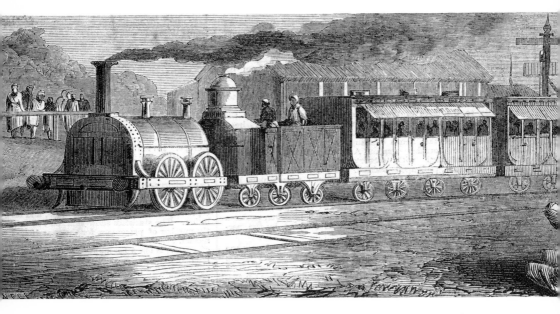

The railways helped to unite the vast subcontinent of India and established new transportation routes.

built to span only 3.2 km of river. By 1900 India had a railway network of 40,233 km and it became a profitable source of income for the Government of India.

The Victoria Railway Terminus in Bombay was one of the most splendid railway stations ever built. It symbolized the solid Victorian confidence of the Raj. Opened in 1887, it looked more like the Houses of Parliament in London than a place where trains stopped. Lady Dufferin, the viceroy's wife, judged it as 'much too magnificent for a bustling crowd of railway passengers.'

Rail travel helped to unite a country separated by deserts, mountains, rivers, jungles and vast plains. Coal, which was used for power in new factories, was transported directly from the mines to the industrial centres. Railways also ensured that the army could move troops speedily from one part of the country to another in the event of another rebellion.

Many times during the nineteenth century India suffered from terrible famines. The railways made it possible for food to be sent to stricken areas. The railways also carried generations of new visitors to the army barracks, tea plantations, missions and remote districts of India.

4 A KIND OF EXILE

Many Europeans found India an uncomfortable place to visit. The weather was extremely hot, and dysentry and malaria were common diseases. The bright colours, spicy foods, unusual insects and intruding snakes were all unfamiliar sights. But the British did not come to India as tourists, they came as rulers. The question as to how long they should rule, continued to bother those who made decisions about India. Harcourt Butler (1869–1938), a trusted adviser on Indian affairs, opposed any statement about the eventual goal of British rule. 'I would take it that it is good enough for us, in the words of the *Te Deum*, (a Latin hymn of thanksgiving sung at services in the Church of England) to govern them and lift them up forever.'

A view of the British settlement in Calcutta – a favoured city amongst the settlers who came to India.

Following the Sepoy Mutiny, British opinion about Indian people had hardened. Pride and a strong sense of duty inspired a new sense of imperialism. Sir Bardle Frere (1815–1884), the British commander who suppressed the Mutiny and was later Governor of Bombay, wrote in 1868: 'You can have little idea how much India has altered. The sympathy which Englishmen felt for the natives has changed to a general feeling of repugnance.'

Missionaries

From the beginning of the nineteenth century, the British saw the Raj as a crusade for Christianity. *The Times* correspondent in India, William Howard Russell, observed with some sarcasm: 'The favourites of heaven, the civilizers of the world (Christians) . . . are naturally the most intolerant in the world.'

As a result of the Sepoy Mutiny of 1857, distrust arose between the settlers and the Indian people and many Europeans decided to leave India.

A group of missionaries and the Indian people they wished to convert at Batala in the Punjab.

The first Baptist missionary was William Carey (1761–1834) who arrived in India in 1794. By 1814 he had established twenty missions throughout the country. Because the new converts were offered a free meal along with religious instruction, they were usually known as 'curry and rice Christians.'

Missionaries had to learn Indian languages if they were to teach the Gospel. This led them to take an interest in Indian education generally. Alexander Duff (1806–1878) founded the Scottish Churches Colleges and the Madras Christian College which became famous for the quality of its teaching. Ambitious Indians soon realized the advantage of having an English education from a missionary school—it was easier to get a job working in some branch of government administration. The missionaries also managed to reform some of the Hindu customs which they disagreed with, such as infanticide (the killing of unwanted children) and suttee (the practice of a widow throwing herself on the

Members of a British community in India early in the twentieth century. Many Europeans became ill and found it difficult to cope with the hot climate.

funeral pyre of her dead husband.) By 1930 only two per cent of India had converted to Christitianity. Missionaries, like British politicians, discovered that the religious ideas and traditions of Hindus and Muslims were equally as strong as their own.

One of the most beneficial legacies of the missionaries to India was the advancement of Indian women. Women were taught how to read and write and they took up places as midwives, nurses, and doctors in the medical colleges which were founded by missionaries.

Memsahibs

The women who came to India from Britain to be with their husbands were known as memsahibs. They brought with them as much furniture and personal belongings as the shipping companies would allow. They also carried to India some of England's more snobbish social ideas. It was said that after passing through the Suez Canal every English-woman became a duchess.

The British memasahibs had little to do each day but recline in the shade and let others wait upon them.

Boredom filled a memsahib's many leisure hours. The day began energetically enough with an early morning horse ride but the rest of the day had no clear purpose. Indian servants bought and prepared the food and did all the household chores. Most of a memsahib's day was spent writing long letters home and reading. After lunch, which was called tiffin, she would rest through the long afternoon. If she had children she did not raise them, they were usually sent to expensive boarding schools in England to be educated.

The ICS
India was governed by a British middle class that sometimes liked to believe it was part of the aristocracy. After 1853, stiff competitive examinations were introduced for people who wished to join the Indian Civil Service (known as the ICS). Candidates also had to know how to ride a horse! Oxford and Cambridge Universities provided a majority of the successful candidates and most were also educated at an English

British officers, the product of the English public school system, having dinner in a mess tent in Mysore.

Many of the young men who came to India hoped life would be one long round of drinking whisky and smoking cigars in gentlemen's clubs. Some did not realize quite how much work was involved.

public school. At the end of the nineteenth century, these schools became enthusiastic supporters of the idea of the Empire. They encouraged young people to think of serving in India and the Empire as a patriotic and moral duty.

A member of the ICS began his career in India as a district officer. He went to an area almost five times larger than Britain, inhabited by millions of people. His main duties were to maintain law and order, settle legal disputes, try criminals and collect taxes. The young graduates who came to India were surprised and sometimes unprepared for the amount of work they had to do. One young magistrate posted in northern India sat hearing criminal cases: 'Though familiar with every refinement of falsehood, he still constantly found himself baffled and quite uncertain what to do. Justice was so passionately demanded, but seemed so rarely obtained, so hard to give, and so little deserved. Yet justice was one of the very things that the English were supposed to have given India.'

Indians suffering from the results of famine. Although the British presence in India seemed to be acceptable to the Indian people, the continued poverty and deprivation of many of them turned them against their rulers.

A member of the ICS regularly toured his district and drew maps which showed who owned various sections of land. These maps were used to assess taxes and were extremely important as the taxes, known as land revenue, mainly paid for British rule. A successful member of the ICS would expect, after a few years, to leave his district to join the provincial judicial service or the Political Department, which guided Indian Princes on how to govern their states. The top jobs were in the Government of India. A member of the ICS might be asked to advise the viceroy or join a legislative council to assist in the political education of Indian people. Every member of the ICS received a good pension when he retired.

The Raj worked reasonably well so long as it was accepted by the Indian people. But in the twentieth century Indian opinion became more and more critical of the Raj as the idea of self-government began to take root in the minds of the people.

5 INDIAN NATIONALISM, 1885–1919

The Indian National Congress

Prime Minister Gladstone's belief in self-government still had great influence in Britain in the 1880s. When applied to India it raised the question of how democratic the Raj actually was. Neither the viceroy nor the Indian Civil Service were elected: the effective rulers of India held their positions of authority by appointment. If British rule was to avoid the criticism of being a tyranny, some means had to be found to bring the Government of India closer to Indian opinion.

William Ewart Gladstone, who was prime minister of Britain four times between 1868 and 1894.

Hence, Britain set out to win the support of educated Indians who were profiting from British rule.

The political organization known as the Indian National Congress was partly the idea of the liberal-minded Octavian Hume (1829–1912), a former member of the ICS who believed that the Raj was becoming an insensitive bureaucracy. He wrote to the viceroy, Lord Dufferin (1826–1902): 'The whole tone of administration is growing rotten. I listen to men talk—Alas! In too many cases, the old desire to have right done, for the love of justice and of God, has melted into a determination to prove the [Indian Civil] Service right.'

In 1885 the Indian National Congress met for the first time in Bombay. Made up of lawyers, teachers and newspaper editors, its members met once a year to discuss political and social issues in a spirit of moderation and friendliness. Lord Dufferin called it 'neither very dangerous

Lord Curzon, an autocratic and controversial viceroy, aggravated the tension between Hindus and Muslims by deciding to divide Bengal in 1904.

The visit of King George V, Emperor of India, and his Queen to Delhi in 1911.

nor very extravagant.' In fact, three Englishmen, including Hume, were chosen as presidents of the Congress in the next fifteen years. During this time, the Congress grew by forming local branches throughout the country. Though its numbers were small, it rapidly became India's most important political organization.

The Muslim League

The Indian National Congress was led by Hindus and this led to suspicion amongst the Muslim community. Hindus outnumbered Muslims by three to one in India and Muslims feared that Hindus would use the Indian National Congress to dominate them. This would not have been difficult as Muslims were generally less educated, poorer, and more politically disorganized than Hindus. The Muslim leader, Sayyid Ahmed Khan (1817–1898), opposed Muslim participation in the Congress and advised Muslims to acquire an English education. He founded the Muslim University of Aligarh, and inspired the Muslim League which was formed in 1906.

The aim of the Muslim League was the advancement of Muslim interests. Muslims lived mainly in the northern provinces of Bengal, the Punjab, and the North-West Frontier. They believed that by co-operating with the British they would receive protection from Hindu domination.

The partition of Bengal

The rivalry between Hindus and Muslims was aggravated by the decision of the viceroy, Lord Curzon (1859–1925), to divide Bengal into two provinces. Bengal had a population of seventy-eight million at the turn of the century. The relatively prosperous Hindus, who were also politically active, lived in western Bengal, while the poorer Muslims lived in the east. After touring the province in 1904, Lord Curzon launched his policy of partition, supposedly in order to simplify the administration of the area. In reality, he wanted to weaken a province which had been critical of British rule. By dividing Bengal he asserted Britain's authority to do whatever it wanted. He also hoped to reduce the political influence of Hindus in Bengal and show Muslims that Britain truly intended to safeguard their interests. Curzon explained: 'The Bengalis... like to think themselves a nation... and dream of a future where the English will have been turned out... If we are weak enough to yield to their clamour now, we shall not be able to dismember or reduce Bengal again.'

The Indian National Congress, led by G. K. Gokhale (1866–1915), launched the first popular Indian protest against British rule. People were persuaded to boycott British cloth in a movement known as the *swadeshi* movement. A *hartal*, or religious day of mourning, was

The elephant at the head of the Dasahra procession in Calcutta salutes King George V and Queen Mary, as part of the Durba celebrations during the royal visit to India in 1911–12.

organized on 16 October 1905. Shops remained closed, students refused to sit their examinations and write on imported paper, women refused to buy foreign bangles, and children gave up sweets.

Lord Curzon was well-known for his arrogance and pomposity. He refused to give up his plan, for it had long been his aim to destroy the Indian National Congress. As early as 1900 he wrote: 'My own belief is that the Congress is tottering to its fall, and one of my great ambitions while in India is to assist it to a peaceful demise.'

After the resignation of Lord Curzon and the return to British Government of the Liberal Party in 1905, the proposed partition of Bengal was dropped. The episode succeeded in showing, however, that Indians could make the imperial government respond to popular feeling. It was in the spirit of co-operation that India supported Britain during the First World War (1914–18). Nearly one million Indians joined the various expeditionary armies, a large number going to France, Egypt and Mesopotamia. Between 1916 and 1917 India recruited 113,000 combatants and 276,000 between 1917 and 1918. India purchased seventy-five million pounds of war bonds, and leaders of the Indian National Congress supported and aided the war effort. Mohandas Gandhi (1869–1948), who had recently returned from South Africa where, as a lawyer, he had been defending Indian rights, helped to recruit Indian soldiers. But the mood of rising Indian expectations after the war was upset by the tragic events in the holy city of Amritsar, which shocked India and the world.

Amritsar

After war ended, in 1918, India reasonably expected greater political freedom. One of US President Wilson's Fourteen Points had stated that an aim of the war should be the self-determination of people: a nation should be free to choose the government it wished. This idea was one of the most important principles used at the Paris Peace Conference in 1919 for creating new countries in eastern Europe from the defeated German and Austro-Hungarian Empires.

The Government of India was cautious as to whether this principle should be applied to India. Worried by the growing dislike of British rule among young Indians, the Rowlatt Acts were passed in 1919. These acts allowed the Government of India to continue the emergency powers which had been introduced during the war. These powers suspended normal legal rights.

The Acts led to protests throughout India and, as during the agitation against the partition of Bengal, a *hartal* was called. There was rioting and some people were murdered. In the Punjab, General Dyer was called upon to restore law and order, which he did by placing a ban on all public meetings. On 13 April 1919, at six o'clock in the evening,

General Dyer ordered his troops to fire at an unarmed crowd in Amritsar on 13 April, 1919. His brutal action angered many people in India and in Britain.

an unarmed crowd of several thousand, who had not heard about the ban, gathered in the walled garden of Jallianwala Bagh in Amritsar. General Dyer ordered his troops to fire on the crowd. Altogether 379 people were killed and 1,000 wounded. The General finally gave the order to stop firing because ammunition was running low. '1,650 rounds were fired, fire being directed on crowds not individuals, and redirected from time to time where the crowds were thickest.'

Though dismissed from the army, General Dyer received £26,000, from a special fund raised by subscribers in Britain and among Europeans in India. Both Dyer's actions and this fund caused anger throughout India and a new leader came forward to condemn British rule more forcefully than ever before. Gandhi became leader of the Indian National Congress in 1920. He led the cry for independent self-government, or *swaraj*, within a year.

6 GANDHI'S ERA

Mahatma

From 1920 to 1934 Mohandas Gandhi emerged as one of the most famous men of the twentieth century. He became known as the Mahatma or great soul, and was admired throughout the world for his simplicity and tolerance. Born into the merchant caste (the name Gandhi means grocer), his intense opposition to British rule was a mixture of the holy man's search for truth and the shopkeeper's ability to add up. British rule would end, he suggested, when the cost of governing India was greater than the profit. Though Gandhi graduated as a lawyer in London in 1891, religious and ethical ideals dominated his life.

Gandhi changed the character of the Indian National Congress when he became president in 1920. Under his leadership the party began to represent India's suffering millions. Gandhi argued that British rule was wrong because so many Indians were crushed by poverty. He wrote that: 'The law in British India is carried on for the exploitation of the masses.'

A young Cambridge graduate, Jawaharlal Nehru (1889–1964), India's first prime minister, was inspired by Gandhi's message that politics must be concerned with the needs of the poor. 'Looking at them [the poor villagers] and their misery and overflowing gratitude, I was filled with shame and sorrow, shame at my own easy-going and comfortable life and our petty politics of the city which ignored this vast multitude of semi-naked sons and daughters of India.'

Gandhi called on Indians to prepare themselves for independence by boycotting British cloth and learning how to spin and weave by using old-fashioned hand looms. He called homespun cloth 'the livery of freedom'. Gandhi spun cloth for half-an-hour every day of his life and fasted on Monday which was also his day of silence.

Gandhi's principles of nonviolence and noncooperation led to campaigns of civil disobedience. Gandhi believed the Raj would end when Indians showed they no longer needed British rule. He called on his followers not to attend British schools, buy British goods, accept public office, attend trials in British courts or pay any taxes. The campaign gained wide success in 1922, but was then ended by Gandhi when a crowd attacked a police station in Chauri Chaura and killed twenty-two policemen.

Many people in India suffered from famine and poverty. Mohandas Gandhi believed that British rule did nothing to help them.

Gandhi defied the British government by walking 322 km to Dandi to collect salt deposits.

The prisoner

In 1922 Gandhi was arrested and sent to gaol. He called prison his temple because it was a place where he practised self-purification. 'Gaol for us is no gaol at all when the whole of India is a prison.' At his trial Gandhi said that Indians were morally superior to the physically more powerful British. But Indians had to learn to act as an independent people. 'Nonco-operation is a protest against an unwitting and unwilling participation in evil. It is not so much British guns that are responsible for our subjection as our voluntary co-operation.'

In 1930 Gandhi opposed the British Government's tax on salt by walking 322 km to Dandi to collect deposits of salt at the seaside. The march took twenty-four days, which was long enough to gather a large group of followers. It also aroused the curiosity of the world's press. Gandhi was arrested because it was illegal to gather free salt in British India.

The epic fast

In 1932, while in prison, Gandhi began his 'epic fast'. He wanted low-caste Indians, the untouchables, to be given the same political rights as other Hindus. The British Government changed its policy and when Gandhi again proposed a fast of twenty-one days the following year, he was released. His prestige in India and throughout the world was so great that no one in authority wished to risk the blame for his death. However, during the years of Gandhi's rise to prominence, Britain remained unwilling to leave India.

Pakistan and Mr Jinnah

Gandhi's popularity was a source of worry to many Muslims. The Hindu character of his ideas and the excitement created by the civil disobedience campaigns made Muslims fearful. They believed Gandhi was inspiring Hindus with a religious fanaticism which would eventually turn on the Muslim community. It was the stated purpose of the Raj to govern in the interests of the whole country and maintain law and order and the friction caused by Gandhi's ideas and methods led the British to believe that India was not yet ready for independence.

The Muslims found a leader of exceptional skill in Mohammed Ali Jinnah (1876–1948). Like Gandhi, Jinnah was a lawyer trained in London. Wealthy, reserved and irreligious, he described the Muslims in India as caught in a no-man's land between the British Empire and Hindu nationalism. He was a bitter opponent of Gandhi and his civil disobedience tactics. He mocked Hindu reverence for the cow with the remark: 'Hindus worship the cow, I eat it.'

Jinnah rejected the Indian National Congress. Instead he built up the Muslim League and turned to the British Government for support.

He persuaded Muslims to co-operate with the British. A brilliant negotiator, he believed that when self-government eventually came he would be able to convince Britain to treat Muslims as a separate nation. In 1940 he announced that Muslims should have a state of their own—Pakistan—made up of provinces where Muslims were in a majority.

Mohammad Jinnah, the Indian Muslim statesman who campaigned for the partition of India into separate Hindu and Muslim states.

*Tear gas being used to disperse a gathering of the Muslim League
meeting to campaign for a separate Muslim nation.*

The Empire strikes back

Britain was sympathetic to Muslim arguments because Gandhi was
disliked and distrusted by the British. Though he preached nonviolence, his campaigns led to violence as crowds got out of control.
In 1931 King George V reacted against inviting Gandhi, 'with no proper
clothes on and barekneed', to tea at Buckingham Palace: 'What! Have
this rebel fakir (a naked holy man) in the Palace after he has been
behind all these attacks upon my loyal officers?'

Thousands of Indian troops fought for the Empire during the First World War. Indian gunners are seen here helping to defend Egypt against the Turks.

No one in the British Government wanted to see the end of the Raj in the two decades after the First World War. This was because India gave Britain a belief in herself, as a great power and as a leading nation in the world. India employed an army of almost 200,000 men, was a source of active trade, and encouraged Britain to maintain naval bases throughout the East. The Secretary of State for India from 1924 to 1928, Lord Birkenhead (1872–1930), said that if Britain lost India it would be a 'tragedy of inconceivable magnitude.'

Even Britain's enemies believed India gave the mother-country confidence. Hitler (1889–1945) wrote in *Mein Kampf*,: 'It is childish to assume that in England the importance of the Indian Empire for the British world view is not appreciated.' In 1940 the most outspoken opponent against ending British rule was made war leader. Winston Churchill (1874–1965) later said he had not become prime minister to witness the end of the Raj.

7 THE TRANSFER OF POWER, 1940–1947

Quit India

In August 1941 Churchill met the United States President, Franklin D. Roosevelt, on board the *Augusta* at Placentia Bay, off Newfoundland, for their first wartime conference. The President suggested, even though the United States had not yet entered the war, that a joint declaration of war aims should be made to mark the historic meeting. This declaration was known as the Atlantic Charter. One of the principles announced in the Charter was that people should freely choose the form of government they wanted. This promised democracy to the countries of Europe overrun by Nazi Germany.

Franklin Delano Roosevelt (1882–1945) who was elected President of the United States on four occasions.

Sir Winston Churchill, the British statesman and war leader, was noted for his opposition to Indian self-government.

The Indian Congress Party meeting to discuss the problem of the Hindu–Muslim antagonism.

The Atlantic Charter was extremely important to India. Because the Indian National Congress did not support or elect the Government of India, it could be said that the Indian people were being governed against their will. The pressure of war forced the British Government to state that India would be granted self-government after the war, though what this really meant remained uncertain. Roosevelt, highly critical of British imperialism, wrote to Churchill in April 1942 to suggest that something should be done immediately.

'American public opinion cannot understand why, if there is a willingness on the part of the British Government to permit the component parts of India to secede [separate] after the war from the British Empire, it is unwilling to permit them to enjoy during the war what is tantamount to [the same as] self-government.'

This was at a time when Japanese armies, at war with Britain and her allies, had overrun Burma and planned to invade India. With the enemy at the gates of India, the Indian National Congress wanted to defend its own country. Disappointed by the offer made by Sir Stafford Cripps in his mission to secure agreement on dominion status for India for after the war, earlier in the year, Gandhi launched his last major campaign of civil disobedience, the 'Quit India' movement of August 1942. He said that Britain, 'India's immediate aggressor', should leave an independent India to defeat the Japanese. The night before the 'Quit India' movement began all the members of the Indian National Congress executive committee, including Gandhi and Nehru, were arrested.

Their arrest caused widespread disorder throughout India. Government buildings, police stations and railway lines were destroyed. Over 1,000 people were killed and 60,000 were arrested. The viceroy, Lord Linlithgow (1887–1952), compared the violence to the Sepoy Mutiny: 'I am engaged here in meeting by far the most serious rebellion since that of 1857, the gravity and extent of which we have so far concealed from the world for reasons of military security.'

Though the Raj was beginning to doubt its ability to govern, it remained as opposed to Gandhi as ever. At this time the Indian leader was described as 'the world's most successful humbug' and 'the Hitler of Indian politics'. When he began his twenty-one day fast in prison in February 1943, the war cabinet refused to release him. Churchill said that to let Gandhi out of prison in the hope that he would call off his fast was likely 'to bring our whole government in India and here at home into ridicule'. An Indian doctor saved Gandhi from certain death by adding glucose to his lime juice drink on the critical twelfth day.

The Mahatma (Mohandas Gandhi) played a major part in India's struggle for home rule and was frequently imprisoned by the British for organizing acts of civil disobedience.

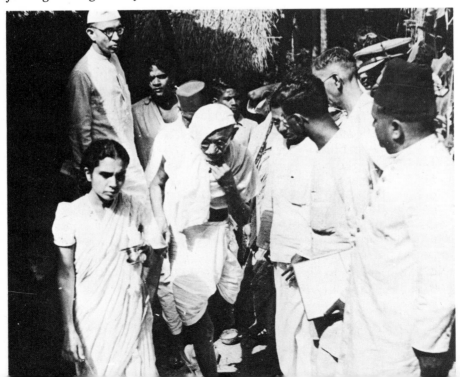

In 1943 Bengal suffered a severe and cruel famine which caused the deaths of more than 600,000 people.

Bengal famine

One of the effects of the Japanese occupation of Burma and Malaya was that India was cut off from supplies of food. In 1943 there was severe famine in Bengal. In the last six months of that year, about 678,000 people died as a result of the famine. The failure of the winter rice crop and the fact that India continued to sell food to other countries left the population of Bengal starving. As food prices rose steeply, farmers did not bring their produce to market because they believed prices would rise even higher. The famine became worse: one estimate put the number of deaths due to the famine as high as two million. The government administration during the famine was found 'utterly inefficient and soft in every respect'.

The new viceroy, Lord Wavell (1883–1953), a famous but tired general, complained in letter after letter to the war cabinet in London that food should be sent immediately. Tons of food waited in Australia, but the war cabinet was unwilling to arrange the shipping. The viceroy confided to the Secretary of State for India in London: 'I feel that many of our troubles in India, both administrative and political, are due to the ignorance and prejudice among your colleagues. It is discouraging work to serve an obviously hostile cabinet, who seem to have no confidence at all in my judgement on any matter.' It was only when Lord Mountbatten (1900–1979), Supreme Allied Commander in South East Asia, wrote to London saying that the food ration to the fighting soldiers would have to be cut, that the war cabinet agreed in 1944, to send shiploads of food to India.

The Bengal famine showed that British interests and Indian needs were not the same. Other signs appeared during the war which suggested that the Raj would not be able to continue. The war prevented the recruitment of new members to the ICS. It was even difficult to find someone suitable to accept the position of viceroy in 1943. Most significantly, because India contributed taxes for the war, Britain owed a large debt to India—£260 million for 1942–3 alone. Towards the end of 1944, Churchill wrote in despair to Roosevelt that Britain had no more funds. The country could not afford to rebuild its own country without loans from the United States. In 1945 the Raj seemed an expensive luxury which Britain could no longer afford. As Lord Wavell described it: 'His Majesty's Government has no longer the power to take effective action.'

Labour in power

In July 1945 the Labour party led by Clement Attlee (1883–1967) dramatically beat Winston Churchill and the Conservative Party in the general election. For the first time in British history the Labour Party had a clear majority. The Labour Party's election manifesto stated that British policy was to leave India as soon as possible. Socialists thought that the Indian Empire belonged to an outdated conservatism.

The Labour Party led by Clement Attlee (below) came into power in Britain in 1945, after beating the Conservative Party in the general election.

Mohammed Ali Jinnah (left), President of the Muslim League, pictured with Sir Stafford Cripps, President of the Board of Trade, in New Delhi, in 1946.

They wanted to get on with reconstructing Britain and to allow the Indian people to develop their own economy and society. Modern Britain had lost the will to be an imperial power. As Churchill later claimed: 'I could have defended the British Empire against anyone, *anyone*, except the British.'

Prime minister Attlee took charge of the Government's Indian policy. He devised a policy which reflected his personality—modest but effective. Britain had no fixed ideas about how self-government should come about. The Indian people had to decide things for themselves. The purpose of British policy was to help Hindus and Muslims reach an agreement. He wrote to the Foreign Secretary, Ernest Bevin (1881–1951): 'We are seeking to fulfil the pledges of this country with dignity and to avoid an ignominious scuttle [an undignified and hurried withdrawal]. But a scuttle it will be if things are allowed to drift ... We are determined to hand over as a going concern and this is precisely what we are making clear to the Indians and we are placing responsibility on their shoulders.'

Getting the Indian political leaders to accept independence proved more difficult than expected. For two years, from 1945 to 1947, it was impossible to get the Muslim League and the Indian National Congress to agree on anything. Their inability to compromise delayed Indian independence. To find a way out of the deadlock, Attlee chose the King's cousin, a man of great personal charm, to be the last viceroy.

8 THE LAST VICEROY

L ord Louis Mountbatten arrived in India in March 1947. He was handsome, confident, frank, with a reputation of being something of a playboy as well as a socialite—altogether an unusual and brilliant choice. He had the ability to bring out the best in other people. His attractive wife, Edwina, had a passionate and sympathetic nature which won her the admiration of Nehru and the people of India. One day Edwina was placed between Nehru and Jinnah to be photographed by the world's press. Jinnah suggested a title for the picture: 'A rose between two thorns.' The Mountbattens brought with them a genuine interest in Indian life and culture, something that could not be said of many others who came to India.

Lord Louis Mountbatten was sent to India in an attempt to ease the worsening situation.

Lord and Lady Mountbatten proved to be very popular figures with the Indian people.

Before Lord Mountbatten left London, King George VI wrote: 'Is he to lead the retreat out of India or is he to work for the reconciliation of Hindus and Muslims?' As it happened he did neither. It suited the new viceroy to pretend that he had complete authority to do what he thought best. He announced that June 1948 would be the date for the withdrawal of British forces. This date was meant to put pressure on Indian political leaders to come to some agreement.

The last Viceroy of India, Lord Mountbatten (left) chats with Jinnah, President of the Muslim League.

The problems

Mountbatten faced three difficult problems in relation to India. For the past two years violence between Hindus and Muslims had been tearing the country apart. 'The situation is everywhere electric,' wrote the viceroy. Every week riots which took place in many cities spread to the countryside. In the Punjab alone some 5,000 people were killed between March and August 1947. The viceroy, of course, tried to stop this violence, but he refused to let British forces be responsible for maintaining the peace once Britain left. As Mountbatten put it: 'British forces would not be available to interfere with disorder.' Britain was leaving India and it could not become a permanent police force. The viceroy's problem was how to end the Raj without Britain being accused of running away in the event of civil war.

A decision also had to be taken on whether or not independence should be granted to a united or divided India. Should power be transferred to the Indian National Congress which was dominated by Hindus, or should India be partitioned, that is divided into two nations according to where Hindus and Muslims were in the majority? The Muslim League led by Jinnah refused to compromise on Pakistan, even though this new country was to be separated by the Himalayas. Jinnah used the present rioting as evidence that the two communities could not live in harmony. Peace, he insisted, would return to India only when Muslims lived in their own country, Pakistan. Jinnah was, in fact, a master at saying no. This led the viceroy to comment, 'My God, he was cold.'

It was one thing for Britain to want to leave India and quite another for the Indian political leaders to agree to accept responsibility for ruling the country. How could they be convinced to accept an agreement when they had been in the habit of disagreeing about everything for at least twenty years? Yet Britain would not impose a solution. Whatever happened had to be seen to be the result of decisions made by Indian leaders. Mountbatten told a rather pleased Jinnah at one of their first meetings that he 'would not recommend any solution which was potentially unacceptable to the Indian parties.'

The solution

Showing great patience, Mountbatten held meeting after meeting with Gandhi, Jinnah and Nehru. Between March and June he frequently worked up to seventeen hours a day. He carefully prepared his arguments, anticipated the next stage of the discussions, and put as much friendly pressure on the leaders as he could. The Indian National Congress finally accepted partition in June 1947. To satisfy Nehru, the Congress leader, the date for independence was brought forward to 15 August 1947.

Gandhi (right) photographed with Jawaharlal Nehru, the first prime minister of the republic of India.

This was none too soon. The viceroy warned His Majesty's Government that if he had to wait until October 1947 'there would have been a complete breakdown.' Gandhi complimented the viceroy on his 'magic tricks in getting the Congress and Muslim League to agree on anything.' Mountbatten was such a popular figure that Nehru asked him to stay on as the first governor general of independent India.

Independence and partition
The day of 15 August was filled with both comedy and tragedy. During the evening celebrations in Delhi, Nehru made his way through a vast

Many of the 6,000 Muslims who left India for Pakistan in 1947 had to make temporary homes in railway terminals.

crowd of some 600,000 people to the bodyguards surrounding the carriage of the viceroy and his wife. The parade had to be abandoned since the crowds had stopped all traffic. The viceroy could not even see the parade stand. 'Nehru fought his way to the coach,' Mountbatten wrote, 'and climbed in to tell us that our daughter Pamela was safe.' An aide described how Nehru came to his and Pamela's rescue when they were overwhelmed by the crowd: 'Nehru fought like a maniac, striking people right and left. Eventually he removed the topee (hat) from a man who had particularly annoyed him and smashed it over his head.'

Ceremonies were only a little more gracious in Karachi when on 14 August a state procession placed Jinnah and Mountbatten in the leading car and Jinnah's sister and Lady Mountbatten in the next. Troops and police kept back the crowds that lined their route. 'As we turned in at the gates of Government House,' Mountbatten explained, 'Jinnah put his hand on my knee and said with deep emotion: "Thank God I have brought you back alive."'

Gandhi refused to take part in the celebrations. According to Mountbatten: 'He realizes that it would not be possible for us to fit him into the programme in the way in which he would feel himself entitled.' Gandhi announced his decision to spend the rest of his life in Pakistan looking after minorities, something he never did. On 15 August, bitterly disappointed at the division of India, he went to Calcutta where he invited everyone to spend the day fasting and doing extra spinning.

A Pakistan-bound train, packed with terrified Muslim refugees who were leaving India to find a new home.

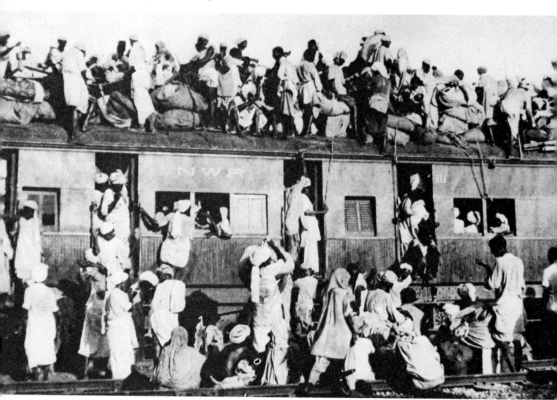

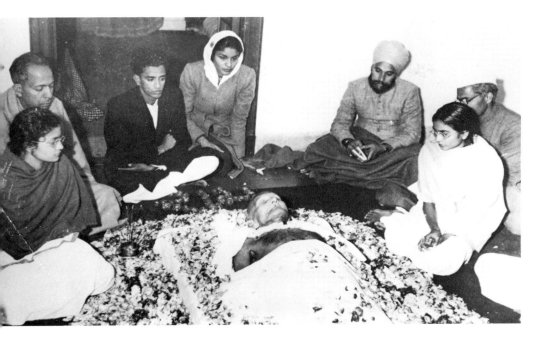

*The body of Mohandas Gandhi lying in state in Birla House in New
Delhi. The great Indian leader was shot and fatally wounded by an
assassin on 30 January, 1948.*

Tragic events followed between the months of August and November
1947, as large numbers of people moved between India and Pakistan.
In the mass migration of people, it was estimated that almost 200,000
were massacred.

But the tragedy of these massacres did not wreck Britain's relationship with India. Lord Mountbatten stayed on until 1948 as governor-
general. India joined the new British Commonwealth and has since
become a voice for the developing countries in Asia and Africa. Nehru,
after he became a world leader, missed the Raj and the heroic days
of India's struggle for freedom. Both Gandhi and Jinnah died in 1948.
Gandhi was murdered at prayers by a Hindu fanatic. Jinnah lived just
long enough to be the first governor general of Pakistan.

The Raj has inspired many books, plays, novels, television pro-
grammes and films. Millions of people with roots in the Indian subcontinent have enriched Britain because they have come here to live
and work.

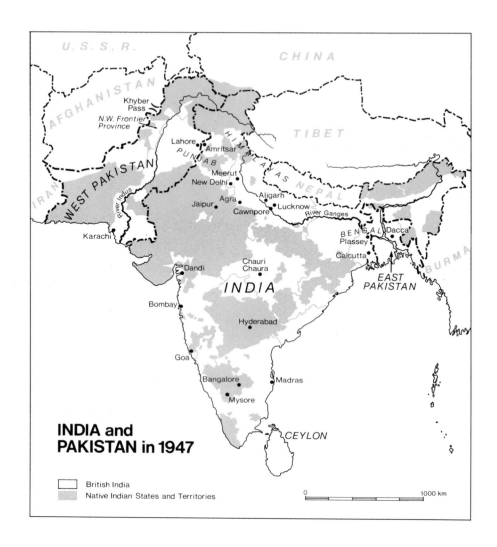

U.S.S.R.

CHINA

AFGHANISTAN

Khyber
Pass

N.W. Frontier
Province

TIBET

Lahore
Amritsar

HIMALAYAS

PUNJAB

WEST PAKISTAN

NEPAL

IRAN

Meerut
New Delhi
Jaipur Agra
Cawnpore

River Indus

Aligarh
Lucknow

River Ganges

BENGAL
Plassey

Dacca

Karachi

Calcutta

Dandi

Chauri
Chaura

INDIA

EAST
PAKISTAN

BURMA

Bombay

Hyderabad

Goa

Bangalore
Madras

Mysore

CEYLON

INDIA and
PAKISTAN in 1947

British India
Native Indian States and Territories

0   1000 km

70

DATE CHART

326 BC	Alexander the Great invades India
1498	Vasco da Gama arrives in India
1600	Queen Elizabeth I of England grants a royal charter to the East India Company
1615	Sir Thomas Roe at the court of the Great Mogul
1707	Death of Aurangzeb, the Great Mogul
1756	Black Hole of Calcutta
1757	Battle of Plassey
1773	Parliament regulates East India Company
1883	Parliament requires East India Company to stop trading
1857	Sepoy Mutiny
1858	The British Government assumes control of India from the East India Company
1876	Queen Victoria made Empress of India
1885	Indian National Congress founded
1906	Muslim League founded The partition of Bengal proposed
1919	Massacre at Amritsar
1922	Gandhi's first great noncooperation campaign in India
1930	Gandhi's salt march to the sea at Dandi
1932	Gandhi's 'epic fast'
1941	Atlantic Charter
1942	'Quit India' movement
1943–4	Bengal famine
1945	Election of the Labour Government in Britain
1947	Lord Mountbatten becomes the last viceroy of India The partition of India into India and Pakistan Independence granted to the two separate nations

GLOSSARY

Caste   Inherited class divisions in Indian society. There are four main castes: priestly, military, merchant and labourer.

Democratic   Something which favours the interests of everyone and benefits all.

Despotic   A form of rule which is both absolute and tyrannical.

Fourteen Points   The principles given by President Wilson in 1918 as war aims of the US.

Harijans   A term Gandhi used for the 'untouchables' which literally means the children of God.

Hartal   The act of closing shops and stopping work as a form of political protest.

Imperialism   The policy of extending the rule of one state over other territories.

Indra   The Hindu god of rain, thunder and lightning often represented riding an elephant and holding a thunderbolt.

Infanticide   A former Hindu custom of killing unwanted children.

Manifesto   The policies stated by a political party.

Memsahib   The name used by the Indian people for European women in India.

Monsoon   A seasonal wind from South Asia that brings extremely heavy rains.

Nabob   A person who returned to England having made a vast fortune in India.

Nationalism   Loyalty or devotion to one's country.

Nawab   Originally a governor in the Mogul Empire, later applied to Muslim noblemen.

Pakistan   Territory in northeast and northwest India which became the independent Muslim nation in 1947.

Raj   Hindi word meaning kingdom and rule. Term given to British rule in India.

Regulate   To bring something under closer control.

Sahib   An Indian word used as a form of address or title after a man's name, used as a mark of respect.

Sanskrit   An ancient Indian language, used nowadays only for religious purposes.

Sepoy   An Indian soldier under British authority.

Sind A region of South East Pakistan, mainly in the lower Indus valley.

Socialists People who believe in State control of the economy, welfare legislation, and the equality of individual wealth.

Subcontinent A large land Mass that makes up part of a continent.

Suttee The custom where a Hindu widow threw herself on the funeral fire of her dead husband.

Swadeshi A term used during the Raj for the policy of boycotting British goods, as part of the campaign for independence.

Swaraj Independence or self-government.

Thuggee Robbers and assassins in India.

Tyranny Oppressive, unjust behaviour or use of authority.

Viceroy of India The head of the Government of India appointed by the British Government.

FURTHER READING

History and Biography

Allen, C. *Plain Tales from the Raj* (Futura, 1977)

Allen, C. *Raj, A Scrapbook of British India 1877–1947* (Penguin, 1977)

Edwards, M. *Red Year, The Indian Rebellion of 1857* (Hamish Hamilton, 1973)

Fischer, L. *The Life of Mahatma Gandhi* (Collins, 1951)

Gibson, M. *The Collapse of Empires* (Wayland, 1986)

Golant, W. *The Long Afternoon* (Hamish Hamilton, 1975)

Hunter, N. *Gandhi* (Wayland, 1986)

Kanitkar, H. *The Partition of India* (Wayland, 1987)

Moorhouse, G. *India Britannica* (Granada, 1987)

Spear, P. *History of India, Volume II* (Penguin, 1970)

Thapar, R. *History of India, Volume I* (Penguin, 1969)

PICTURE ACKNOWLEDGEMENTS

BBC Hulton Picture Library 15, 29, 40; Mary Evans Picture Library 12, 13, 14, 16, 20, 22, 25, 26, 32, 33, 35, 37, 38, 39; Sean Goddard 70; Illustrated London News 8, 68; Mansell Collection 10, 11, 17, 18, 19, 27, 30, 31, 36, 42, 47, 60, 62, 66; Topham Picture Library 9, 43, 45, 49, 52, 53, 55, 56, 57, 58, 59, 61, 63, 64, 69; Wayland Picture Library 21, 23, 24, 28, 34, 41, 67.

INDEX

P2